black trees

Andrew Mossin

SPUYTEN DUYVIL

New York   Paris

ISBN 978-1-959556-18-3

Cover: Hasegawa Tohaku, *Pine Trees* (Shōrin-zu byōbu)

Library of Congress Cataloging-in-Publication Data

Names: Mossin, Andrew, author.
Title: Black trees / Andrew Mossin.
Description: New York : Spuyten Duyvil, [2023]
Identifiers: LCCN 2023000173 | ISBN 9781959556183 (paperback)
Subjects: LCGFT: Poetry.
Classification: LCC PS3563.O8858 B53 2023 | DDC 811/.54--dc23/eng/20230113
LC record available at https://lccn.loc.gov/2023000173

In Memoriam

Ronald Johnson
1935-1988

and hold a candle to
fireworks being raised
sprung daffodil and iris
in golden-purpled robes

Go home where the green bird is—
the trees where you pass
to grass
                    Lorine Niedecker

CONTENTS

standing at the periphery

words turnd in the phrases of song
before our song
                    Robert Duncan

I.

A radicalism
of fate   to face
          one by one—

the days 'upon the
sands'

Reach their magnificent
belt, become the
early & late
morning.

Not a time but
timed to be shown

in late winter
early 'till the tide
went past my simple Shoe'

              ∎

Is water any deeper
than it is here, inside
my left pocket?

A willingness to let
the world go, you said

One follows another.

In some dance, the fiction
is simple. Carry the world
inside your eye. A red

spirit, released, betokening
left to rot as bodies do.

■

All the days are one
day, chronographic time
envelops the space we see
yesterday, not at all the
same, but a window
ajar...the frost pure
and welcome.

'And He – He followed – close behind – '

Not fate but fear
drove through the evening

to ease our soldiered spirit.
Bend? Break?

Slow as one is looking from the hill
sovereign at this distance.

      ■

What gave it pause? Set
down the pencil, placed paper
on a slope, slid down its

mouth—

Not paper or pencil

but my hand, moving
left to right.

The equidistance between far points
of light. One is another's
habit, cut to fit.

Realism grows on the body like this.

Daylight is softer as you enter the cabin, sleek
even when you let its handle break.

On these floors
one is left to startle

as beginning is another
reproof.

                  ■

'The sun is the star of poverty.'

Risk your wares here, then.

At mid-day to cross the sidewalk another way.

Lighter, breaking pace. Eventually
the same spirit that startled you

forward
a bit from here.

In this 'rehearsal of ourselves'
objects that had died
in color, left on the table.

A night drawing, you had no
place to hang it. 'Here, in the
July day, sun—'

As wind, sail, blossom
light of spring.

■

Partnered with no one

to say, kindling, black
sticks, wind...

The hopefulness of solitude
necessary all year

round.

I had come back from those
rounds, beaten the road
when roses, late signs
of life, poured from the
hillside....

Have you a mountain
scene in mind, saying it to oneself

morning noon and night.

               ■

          'So real
we wept'   for nobody
the sea was wetter than we
said it would've been—

Color from a bridge
up north where the division
is less subtle.

Bridge and light, storms
as they come from the east.

To narrate we said it was
here, inside the seams of your
hair, light as it poured once
from a cypress tree.

I am resting where speech
has gone quiet. A scene of
mercy, not intent.

A scene of mercy, not
intent.

■

'God is named at the most
secret core of his absence.'
—Jabès

Ordinary light
passes from inside the house. A will to
exist solely *here*.

The reasoning to become
oneself at all.

Longitudinal
mapping of the inside world.

A day later, the frugal
speech of someone saying

'time.'

II.

Daylight, you and the other-
ness of each instant—
     so worlds are divided

into here & there, the emptiness
of a street at evening
          you and the

sea light, one wants to divulge
so many particulars, as if to abridge

person, make habit a place
to rest.

     ■

I'm carrying no
consequence but this arc
     traced on wood—

sea foam I saw once
at the end of a beach, roped

off, to end there, one's
face averted, mystic shadow

of Carolina coast.

The town center
near where we live—

deserted at dusk. 'I left
to go back to church, but it was darker

than I remembered on Oakland
and the bodies were different.'

As if to ask—
of anyone—

how many days
here…how many are left

out of order?

                    ∎

I am aided in this by memory
of my mother's hands

at sunup, her limp
walk into the light of kitchen.

Mourning doves resting

between pillars, bowed
among poplars

and newly seeded beds
of marigolds.

Dense fog this morning
said the report. One is moving

outside to find it, porous. wind-
chapped, layers of light

revealing objects in a clear
meadow. The yearning for specifics

that is eastern in intent. So many
come back to sit here, light

at dawn, the fog that's passing
or passed.

　　　　　∎

Days are less confrontational.
At the train station in the

mornings, concrete
surfaces bathed in light.

Steel rails. A small
gathering of crows atop the station house.

Turn oneself away
from what it sees. Windless

day begins here.

rites of observation

If breathing is light, the heart is light, for every
movement of breath-energy affects the heart.
  The Secret of the Golden Flower: A Chinese Book of Life
    (tr. Richard Wilhelm)

I.

Letting go—
'smell of sun
on lilac...'

licorice taste in the mouth

'bees browse the lilac'
from yesterday's
                    garden, a blue

shaped bird, apparent, dis-
appearing, less real

to the touch than wire.

                    ■

I am etched
in charcoal. Sweet breath
of mint. High talk
at nighttime...

The year falls back, hangs
in the balance. Weighted
not less than her
eyes—

          to uncover their mirth

in simple plain speech.

What came to uncover us, simple duty, the plan
unplanned....
                    Went out at the late light, with it
got started, held a small bag of groceries
waist high—

recognition of world work, insistent
flower, my being
at peace with whoever

I will become.

                    ■

Perhaps we are going
to rest here. The seasons

'shift – my Picture – '

A brightening between
periods of rain.

And if I went
to Heaven, where would
the crossing be, back
there or underneath

a garden stair?

                ∎

'The different between Despair
And Fear, is like the One
Between the instant of a Wreck
And when the Wreck has been' (1863)

Light struck
at dawn
            winced to see it
flash—

Locusts in mind the dark
lifts slowly

blue on black.

'Light and shade—*images, in the world, of the
correlation of contraries'*

Yesterday the pattern
re-made on sweet red
pages.
        Apprenticeship
is long, the happiness

late when it arrives.

                ■

I don't doubt
the work its place. In the world
a spiritual exercise. Out of its
ward
        'to undergo time and space'

Body travel, young beginnings…

The place we were
when she said there was one to know

apart from oneself.

'I don't doubt
your sincerity'

A passage of speech
as obedience to its frame
is residual as locust
light—

      from the staircase

the moon is not individuated
or patterned
              wall light

switched off   all of it
corridor.

■

The dailiness of tides
from the west. Near Santa Cruz
as a young man

          I took a friend's arm in mine—

Walk back ocean's track
rugged near rock's
             ledge—

the surface   of each wave
tipped with color.

II.

All of which is eventually
moon—
        cropped from the sky

bolder than we remembered
as skin forms a bruise
from night falls.

∎

Not yesterday, but against
ripped calendar time
to inhabit these
solstice days—

Moon is resting, the whites
of their eyes when they
return, sky bird

at dawn.

Our human shelter
impounded—

      water is less & less
tangible, bluer than sky
the real slight to our

habitat, a low wind
from the east, Saturn

bending light eons
from where we are.

    ■

I have skipped
kinship, built a house
of words.

The days come
trustworthy or not

without company
the birds remain merciful

companions.

Plural as mourning
doves the myrtle branches
braver than I

can skip light
from a can of red—

     streaks across an open sky.

    ■

'Border thyme, corn
row asylum'

bidding the world
farewell, an adopted son

no less real
for having burnt

wood in September.

And you.
And you.

'We are living
       parallel lives'

Of witness
at daylight's edge.

III.

The falcons are out. One day
there's a rift of sky

light, teeming with
traces. One by one to scatter

ash the way hawks at noon
fly out of sight. Window

to doorway. The aftermath
of their passing.

Red on black when the light
reappears.

■

Emptiness is a declination
language has given us. To say

'everything surrounded him took shape
also, becoming a recognizable unity'

the severity of movement
registering our adjustment

on broken ground.

As though this
absence—

mouthless   muted
a derangement of the body

at will's door...

'near the window, cut
off by severity, by obduracy, by
sharpness'

       ■

One can't cross the voice
out or eliminate its
humility

To give its testimony
far from the sea

      'vague silver
      tarnished to blue'

Of no promise
but sundown....

Mint from the garden
was weighted in the palms

held to my mother's
eyes. Now the erasure

of her eyes—sympathetic
to the end—bright

daylight companion.

　　　　.

Not named by what it
was but by what it wasn't—

'In the rhythm of its making
I can't say if I hear
　　　　language at all'

　　　　　　　　The low cry of
　　　　　　　　mourning doves, un-

　　　　　　　　sustainable outside
my window.

IV.

You dont see light
Until sensation of seeing light
Is registered in Perception
  Jack Kerouac

    Shells are beads
    thrown into the air.

    Night crown. Sweet
    mint. Table scraps

    at sundown. Lift
    heaven's door. The

    ajar space is
    infinite.

       ■

    As 'Economy'
    loosens the basis

    of where we
    live, outside a small

    driveway, the trees
    encircling, one

    sees rain thru
    each set of limbs.

A year is water.
Another
          rising from earth.

Silver on the sand.

A marge where
skin sloughs off...

          ▪

'I repeated the names
under my breath, breaking
their syllables'

as ivory cloud

as ivy
as ivy cloud

apprehension's call

But it was always the water
the power of flying deep
green rivers cut the rock
rapids boiled down,
a scene of power.
                    Muriel Rukeyser

I.

IF STANDING...

while the rain kept
coming, itself a version

of earlier rainfall—

To adjust sight, sit with one's
thoughts, the closed
over effect

Of nothing of note.

∎

If you name some things
If discs of light

follow into the river
a body follows another

to safety....Human
situatedness, the intricate

number of days, carried
ahead of them.

'A ferocious mumbling in public
of rootless speech'

        ▪

The idea persists, idiomatic
struggle, blown horn
                of trouble—

treble blown clear
            as water enters
    the ground

Not steel but spoken
                through its conduits
        pale where hands can

shelter under falling rock.

'It appeared to me
that the meadow surface
had been heaved by the
frost & then the water
had run down & under
it & finally when the ice
rose lifted it up—'
                    Feb 26th, 1851

Contiguous with this
time, temporality's low
            falling sound—

as if what's seen is
what's heard

'But to whom tell
the silences?

Birdsong at dawn.

'beside banks in water, kame of the
bottom, fish orchards and gardens,

tenements'

■

As language
narrates a garden 1963

the fall of magnolia sweet
mint on the tips of our fingers

white cloth from a window

blown open—

to arrive is to return
against the bottomed-out

site, spare as any
object in daylight.

Ordinance. Black moon.

Yesterday the ellipsis of bodily.

The earth so often
plural, it hands us back

provisional days.

∎

'We never know where
              we are going—

We jest and shut the Door'

Pigeons flitting
out of view, so little

wind, cautionary as flags
flying half-staff

smooth rockcress
blooming in late April sky.

II.

Noticing the back
yard sign, 'empty
trash here'

as sun pitches
its light
across yellow

squares.

                ■

Not ash
but crocus

spring's flower
appearing

on rain-soaked
ground.

Negotiable delays....

Sundown at 5:46.

Curtain itself, a covering
retraced by hand.

■

On earth as
nowhere.   encamped

here as Basho returns
to hear us sing

old music from another
land.

As freezing
outside all winter

cacti lie down in a March
breeze. The collect

of their branches, pronged
leaflets, spare to the touch

in late afternoon.

.

The patterns of sunlight

outside then in
where the steps lead to a garden.

A lone
hawk moves across the line

of low clouds—

winter skies

broken cloud cover.

'The careful branching of light

at dawn, the ceiling a jeweled surface resting
above one's eyes'

Recognition is supple.

A branch from the myrtle outside my window.

Sixteen summers...

A coil of pine
needles

unbending in the palm.

■

Alighting
on a feeder, morning's saffron

sparrow, skin
and bones.

'There was paradise, I saw it at the end
of a river, the beautiful willingness of small
birds, flowers that rose in a line across the
banks, so any child could lose themselves
there, in between the colors, small world
of particulars, gathered again, one by one,
a contract of perfect consanguinity.'

As standing above the water
he may have dreamt once of falling

headfirst, without fear.

ooo

'The pure products....'

Not intelligible here, among daylight's
last sparrows, in a row

on the fence outside
my window.

III.

'Hill of white
flowers, a spring
in place of fields'

Miraculous daylight. Shadow
splinter of the broken
                                    wing.

                    ▪

A world sliding
out of view, un-

tethered.

A form of happiness—

with Reznikoff at our

side, 'No one is on the lawn so early
but the birds...'

■

Phases of the moon...halfway
to full. The partnership

light makes between surface
and object.

Ordinary daylight when the
train moves into a snow squall.

Our location inside
these misremembered days....

'From the fog a gull flies
slowly...'

away from us & into
the darkness.

      ■

      Atonement
is secondary. A wash
of yellow light....

where the perimeter is stained.

Oneself asserting its wants.
Delivering itself of another.

■

The body listens to what it needs.

Bread, it says.
Water.

black trees

The old song is about fear, about
tomorrow and next year.
                    Denise Levertov

Pale bare
limbs...slow-
moving

into
evening.

Light, dripped across
a bird's wing—

day by day

in seriatim....

■

'Image of Light, Adieu—'

bread lost in spring
grass, moldy piece left
for a cardinal

seeking water.

Not remembering
light, the house and
garden, planted with

vegetables—

      where the rocket
launcher was placed
by Russians, she
said....

          ■

      'I can't express to
you how scary. It makes
this sound: *shooh shooh shooh*.
These rocket fly with such
force, and at night they
make these red streaks...'
      (*NY Times*, March 20, 2022)

The particulars not escaping notice....

'The suffering of our time'

'Our gaze turned to the ground.'

A woman walking past the
garden where her husband is buried.

       ■

As if one could
imagine a day without
a day behind it...

Each carrying what they own
on a road heading west.

There are reasons
to gather
            firewood—

for a late spring

How many mouths
to feed, sure sign of
irises
            blackened by spring
frost   in a line

out back.

            ▪

Peony dusk
rises from outside
one garden
            —now two
split halves

of late spring—

One can't resume
what's taken off

the map—

Pre-war he says
no longer
           exists—

'We are common
people now, without
any place'

                ∎

'Orphaned in the fullest sense
of the term, of father and mother, but
also of himself'

No water....sun
minimal...

As light
  combines
objects—

sun dial in the
rain—we said it was
for good luck—

a game of chance

resin on the bow
another's eye

to look us over.

▪

Was 'I' different from
others—produced at what
cost—

Post-war

Diaspora's dark fig
consumed
              out of doors.

As grey skies
this morning   a border
between one roof
& another—

I returned this way year after year
now the 16th summer

following spring—a change
of season—rains then low lying
clouds—northwesterly

winds....

■

Yesterday returning by
SEPTA at 4:43
                        copper & red of the
station in late afternoon

'temperatures will drop sharply
while barometer readings rise'

The next day and the day after that....

'Any day away
from home   is the same
as any day'

What body is it
any of us can keep?

Recorded late spring
today is another
          day in time—

Virgil's calyx in mind.

                ▪

          Tree bank
encircled by mud flat—
pond scum   a change
from yesterday—

light as corridor

here among the living.

To endure 'the lovely
emptiness'   of dawn—

so much patience

'as children remain
behind'   faceless in their
return

& changeless

      'under foreign skies'

    ■

Ecliptic angle of moon
on basin—

red break of dawn
we can see   so many

in one   Eternal
habit of return

to fold one flower
over another—

ailanthus root
moved to the center

of vision.

The possible world
resituated as tale—

    'I held onto your
hand all the way'

A prayer formed from dreams.

      ∎

As leaning over the kitchen
sink   my mother's sheer

night dress   all day near
my heart

Blue surface of her
robed
      saffron skin

Pale water on the surface of each
extended

hand.

spirit's route

We understood only this,
Having no hold on anything else.
The Lotus Sutra (tr. Leon Hurvitz)

I.

At any point in the journey
       what's light   or dark

simpler to ask

where the garden is   a border
of cacti   last season's

geraniums   seedlings

waiting   new ground.

      ■

The dead in heaven
lighter than our beings

governed by dialogue   from the stars

A change is coming   daylight to
night soil

      As I remember the road
back to town   September   the early

days passing over us
      retreat to a shady spot.

Each hour   can we
say the same
        thing—

slope green   to build
a river inside it

'My heart's in the highlands'

recovered out of another time

'winking
        air   headlights'

springtime air

        ■

'In March a little redbreast came back'

Passing facts

sticks & twine

nests   damp ground   at once
removed   and in

place

                Spiked lobelia
in the distance
                    so many walking

out to the edge   Hudson waters

my lord of hosts
                        so many
waking   without partners

            ■

To hear them sing again
chance recording

A clean white sheet   hanging
over the lawn
                    billowing out—

Each occasion less than one
more than two   each

break time   a simple
method
                to keep honest.

Not a care
in the world.

Debts for all
to see.

Late sky. Last
for a while.

A deal for any
time.

▪

        As hunger is   a version
of reality   encountered here too   in the thick of
it   another one waiting

to hear us out.

        'Let every star remain above & beyond...'

II.

Disturbed   awake near the end
of a dream

          'You weren't resting but moving
about'

Ordinary life   resists any
name   all we cannot

see   resting by a river
in springtime

          ■

Pulled back to reveal   a garden
once the emptied-out   shell of its owner

fir & conifer in the distance   one is left
ashamed   to come without

sorrow or care   curious

the objects   scattered over raked
ground

As any of us   inside

the light   makes way

to others   all night

    wind outside   in the

morning   how many birds
                          rendering song?

A car passing

east toward town…

A river located elsewhere
moving into view.

               ■

Across the sill   light separating each
finger pressed into wood.

The leaves outside
floating, curling into

insignia.

Now & again

       each black letter

rises....

Composition is light.

'the prunings   burn them'

Outside with them   weather
passing storms
                coming from the west.

■

Black April stars
                descending the stairs

kneeling at the lip of each
iron gate.

III.

             None to follow
ideas in things   realism's

slow movement   outside
shifted here
                  among blooming

apple   pink & white
cherry blossoms

        loosened by wind

        ■

As any returns
to a core dream

of garden earth   winding
back in time

'And grass with grass
....faceless as the grass'

       As any name
is given   twice—

Bread on the table
for spring supper

      —let us eat, o lord

lapsed circuit

The dead have their own tasks.
Rilke.

As any can be alone
here   shelled curtains   blowing

into the room   over her desk
as kite string   pulled tight

from a woman's hand   the borderland

she said   is here   the border
land   is open

for all to see...

■

Pulled under

wave after wave   when did our mother
appear   her body

shaded, shaped
by water   inside its circuit

her lungs drawing air
from water.

Patience—

what we cannot see
the dogwood breaks—white—
pear tree and apple—red

blaze of color

How many days
left inside the orchard

The wild plum tree
branches

broken in a passing storm.

■

A day ahead.
A day behind.

Reading from the pile
to claim old roots....

Years at once   passed
over.   Your letter

tucked in the book
I'd not opened in years.

'The air, light comes
through the room—

scented by fig and lemon.
I'm misremembering

surely, that you were ever
here with me, yet...'

No doubt, the rains across
your yard, pooling

in the spring grass.

∎

As peach tree and plum
        congregate—

not as signatory   but memory
laden   reading them back

into the garden   a sign
of passing   here among the

gray sparrows
                gathered on a single branch

        Will power
estranged from the bodies

of those passed on.

How many days   isolated
in spring

yearning for Pisa   as my father
rested on stone once
                              beside the tower

His face   softened by April light

'I'm not moving from here
but resting my body.'

Terminus of shadow
sliced in two.

                ■

As any belief is
a circle   cut from the

pear tree   by hand

pulled from hardened earth.

'I've got no memory of the days
leading up to this one, the ones before
this one leading into silence.'

Foreground & background—

Blue light, compass air
sweet
       actual sound.

    •

'Be patient, let them come to you.'

Word for word
slopes to the bottom of the sidewalk

in late or early spring

the ponding water
from rainfall
yesterday at 5:33 p.m.

At sundown

      to kneel toward the west

arm-in-arm   companionate
as if listening

      to sirens—

        'the air is full of invisible bolts....'

     ■

        the woods where the light

takes the body   we are leaving the parts out   the body
in transit
        body where the woods are

light the canopy   at rest in

            Heaven's mouth

into the fire

To stretch out, with our feet, and hands too.
Just air.
  Hölderlin (tr. Richard Sieburth)

Reading of the gingko:

'the leaf has a notch at top
and is green above

and palish beneath. The flowers
are borne in clusters

in the second month and are
rarely seen by people....'

Yin hsing (silver apricot)
held to the eye

            'a single branch often
bears tens or hundreds of seeds
resembling the seeds of *lien*.'

Cupped once   in & out
of my hands   the seeds this small

bright to the tongue.

The entropy
of leaves   emptied

by color   wind chimes
at night
                    the squall
passing thru—

'Tonight no open
windows'

So little kept   from view
to see slight changes

one must kneel
in old territory again

Potomac stillness
far south of us.

Saying is doing   here in passage
slipstream of the birds

flight we draw across one   landscape
two birds   across one landscape

two birds at rest   the pattern can
repeat

what isn't   conscious
returns as thought.

Yesterday   standing in the circle
of sunlight
                        I carried cut

flowers—roses & day lilies—
in bunches

and rested them
on a glass table

breaking their stems apart
in fresh water

          'the kernel green when young,
later becoming yellow'

Memento mori   shades of what we recall

transitory as growing trees
here in spring
                    abundant as any

Does the spring come
without call?

                    ∎

Reading again of my mother's
fall in winter (ca. 1966)
                    on ice   three ribs

broken—

                    the ease with which I
slip & carry myself out

from these images   a thought
process
                    like memory but not

Her body   frail   thinner
than I'd recalled
                    resting on a wood porch

swing in late spring...

Linden & poplar & cherry

in a line of vision

outside   a bank of daffodils
yellow   creased

by wind.

Trees rocked by northerly
winds
      channel rock   safe haven

     'Slip your hand
through emptiness   it is still

empty'

Two trees.
One building.

One tree.
Two buildings.

      Two hands above the water.

      Gifts of surface & depth.

So gentle   the daylight
makes room for
                    voices—

'May flower & cowslips'

Held by hand a summons
for your eye.

                    Companionate
days   shelter low wind

at daylight the reunion
of water & earth.

Before an open window   loose as one
body is beside another   the crisis of self
that passes

                    out of doors—

wind   shelter   blue light

                              'they all rush into the fire'

6 February—3 June 2022

coda:
parts of a world

To walk outside is to see back of one's habitat and its enclosure. Similarly, to remain inside and look through a window into daylight is to experience the transiency and mystery of the observable world. The provisional intent is to remain, as best as one does and can, within the spectrum of ongoing and uninterrupted perception, to attend with observance and care to the world as it shows itself in "rites of participation," as Robert Duncan has named them.

For the ancient Greeks, the complexity of inner thought and outer experience found parallels in language that named inner and outer levels of experience. Thus, as Ruth Padel has pointed out in *In and Out of the Mind* through her discussion of language used to describe specific elements of the mind/body experience (e.g. *pherenes* [lungs], *menos* [blood], *psuche* [breath]}: 'No word has a total monopoly over thinking or feeling. Concrete physical organs belong with ideas of psychological agency. Intellectual activity is inseparable from emotional activity."

Poetic thought is inseparable from the emotional activity that precipitates it, whether the connection being made is between present and past or an anterior state of understanding, a prehensile and inchoate perception of past present and future past that occurs at the syntactical and referential levels of language. I am not one but two thoughts/feelings, inseparable from what provoked them, what inscribes them in memory. To resume is to take in what one has already done, re-made, in a shadow play of light and wind and air that are themselves alternate forms of being.

"Why do precisely these objects which we behold make a world?" Thoreau asks in *Walden* in a passage I underlined the first time I read it over 40 years ago (the edition of the book I read in my first year in college is the same one I quote from today). There are no secure answers. The world of waking and the world of the poem are one object. The language that enters and animates both creates the circumstantial position we live through as "rites of participation" as Robert Duncan has described them. The realm of the poem is an inhabited world, populated as much by what we know and see as by what we can't articulate or find the words for.

Alternately watching and being watched, our body is created anew with each repositioning toward this or that seen thing. The world and its objects. The world seen and the world under observation. The purposive drift and draw of the creaturely, non-human world that is integral to what any of us may know or recover. Rocks from the bottom of a garden I have been living near for 16 years. "It is a mirror which no stone can crack, whose quicksilver will never wear off, whose gilding Nature continually repairs," Thoreau writes in another underlined passage. To see the world each day as it is, to live quietly with its surfaces, cracks, repairs. The truth of any day is that it ends where it started.

Most afternoons on my return trip by SEPTA regional rail from a day of teaching at the university where I work in Philadelphia, our train stops just after Link Belt Station in Bucks County to wait for the southbound train to pass. In those minutes, looking out into the late afternoon light you can see rows of maple trees lining the border between the tracks and the open fields beyond. The tree limbs, gnarled black nets in the light, appear weightless and separated from the trees' trunks as they extend out over the ragged yellow grass that grows in clumps near the rail bed. Each afternoon we stop and wait for the southbound train and each afternoon I stare out at the black trees that will be there waiting for me tomorrow and the day after that.

Sky and ground. Sky and ground again. A few evening birds inhabiting the space between.

DOYLESTOWN, PA

10 MAY -29 November 2022

Notes & Acknowledgments

Phrases and words from a number of writers appear throughout this work, including Du Fu, Emily Dickinson, Henry David Thoreau, William Carlos Williams, Charles Reznikoff, Denise Levertov, Muriel Rukeyser, and Robert Duncan.

Thanks to Joseph Donahue for his careful reading of this work as it progressed and for his generous comment that appears on the back cover. As always, I owe Tod Thilleman, a brother-in-arms among these trees, deep gratitude for his ongoing support of my work. And to my wife, Monica, who listens patiently to and keeps daily company with my poems as they are written, this book is for her, in faith and love.